A Child's Garden

A Child's Garden

Introducing Your Child to the Joys of the Garden

by Elizabeth St. Cloud Muse

Illustrated by Eva Saull

LITTLE, BROWN AND COMPANY

BOSTON NEW YORK LONDON

First Edition

ISBN 0-316-60943-9

Designed by Jo Anne Metsch

10 9 8 7 6 5 4 3 2 1

SC-CHINA

Printed in Hong Kong

These are the gardening adventures of

Contents

Introduction

Growing toddlers understand more and more about the world around them each and every day. What they didn't notice last week becomes an object of fascination and a new lesson this week. You can share your love of gardening with your child, expanding your little one's knowledge of the surroundings while capturing the child's attention and imagination.

As my son grows, the wonders of the garden continue to surprise him. I am amazed at how fast the seasons slip by and how much my son learns as they pass. As the garden changes, we share new and different things. Much to my amazement and delight, he will point out birds in the trees that I have missed and run to smell flowers he has never seen before. Instilling a sense of curiosity in your child is a gift that will last a lifetime. At the same time, you will rediscover your own love of nature and all it has to offer.

Clouds

Children love to look at clouds—big fluffy white clouds in the afternoon and striking pink clouds in the evening sky. Lie on a blanket with your child on a bright sunny day and look up. Point out the familiar shapes of rabbits, trucks, and dogs. At first your child will look around for the rabbit you are talking about. Before long, however, your little one will understand that the cloud you are pointing to looks like a bunny from a favorite bedtime story. Soon your imaginations will run wild together.

Clouds in the Sky

Shape   Date

Clouds in the Sky

Shape	Date

Seeds

Planting seeds with your child is an activity that will bring joy in the moment and fresh flowers and vegetables for the table in the weeks to come. Planting flower seeds is a wonderful project for very small children. The precision necessary to sow seeds for a vegetable patch isn't as important with a flowerbed.

Your little one can have fun picking out flowers to plant in favorite colors or choosing plants with funny names. Flowers that germinate quickly are the best. Try sunflowers, zinnias, and cosmos, which grow quickly and flower in profusion. Find a small trowel for your child to help loosen the earth in the garden. Your little one can scatter seeds in the fresh soil or simply have fun playing in the dirt as you plant. If an empty spot magically appears when the garden bursts to life weeks later, it will be a wonderful reminder of the place where your little one sat and played while you gardened together.

Flowerbed Design

SEEDS PLANTED

Flower	Color	Height

Flowerbed Design

S E E D S   P L A N T E D

Flower	Color	Height

Rain

Sitting in a cozy chair and looking out the window together can be a great way to enjoy a rainy day. Little fingers can follow the water as it trails down the glass. Together you can play a game by choosing two raindrops on the windowpane and guessing which one will finish first in a race to the bottom.

If the weather is warm, put on a rain slicker and some galoshes and go outside together. You can watch the water droplets as they bounce off leaves and collect on flower petals. Your child will love jumping in the puddles that form along the garden path. As the shower subsides and the sun shines through millions of raindrops in the distance, look for a rainbow. Describe the colors you see and recount all the old fables about leprechauns and fairies, the secret kingdoms where they live, and the pot of gold they hide at the end of the rainbow.

Counting

You can help your little one learn to count in your everyday adventures about the garden. The garden presents numerous opportunities to make learning numbers fun. Together you can count how many stones are in the path leading to your favorite bench, how many rocks your little one can hold in cupped hands, and how many birds are on the feeder at any given time.

Counting in the Garden

Number   Description

 2 2

Counting in the Garden

Number   Description

 2 3

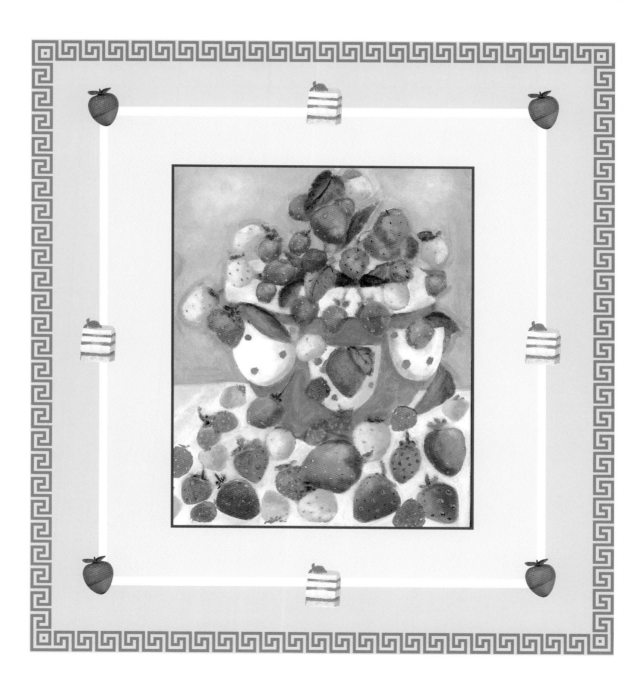

Strawberries

Growing strawberries is a wonderful way to bring homegrown fruit to your table. Strawberry plants are readily available at your local nursery and are quite easy to grow. You and your little one can plant them directly in the garden or use a strawberry pot placed on a terrace or by the kitchen door. Together you can watch as little green strawberries appear and slowly begin to turn red. Inevitably, your enthusiastic child will pick the unripe berries, but because strawberry plants produce quite a bit of fruit, a few missing won't be noticed. Once the strawberries ripen, they can be eaten off the plant as you wander about the garden or taken inside to top cereal, cake, or ice cream.

Garden Party

On a sunny day, while your child takes an afternoon nap, plan an impromptu garden party, inviting all your little one's favorite stuffed animals. Lay down a lovely blanket or bring a small table out for the occasion. Milk and cookies can be the feast and a simple arrangement of flowers picked earlier by little hands can be the centerpiece. Add music to the party, and you and your child will laugh out loud as you dance about the garden with stuffed animals in tow.

Our Garden Party

 ## Guest List

_____   _____

_____   _____

_____   _____

_____   _____

_____   _____

_____   _____

 ## Menu

_____

_____

_____

_____

_____

_____

Our Garden Party

Activities

_____

_____

_____

_____

_____

_____

  ## Special Memories

_____

_____

_____

_____

Date _____

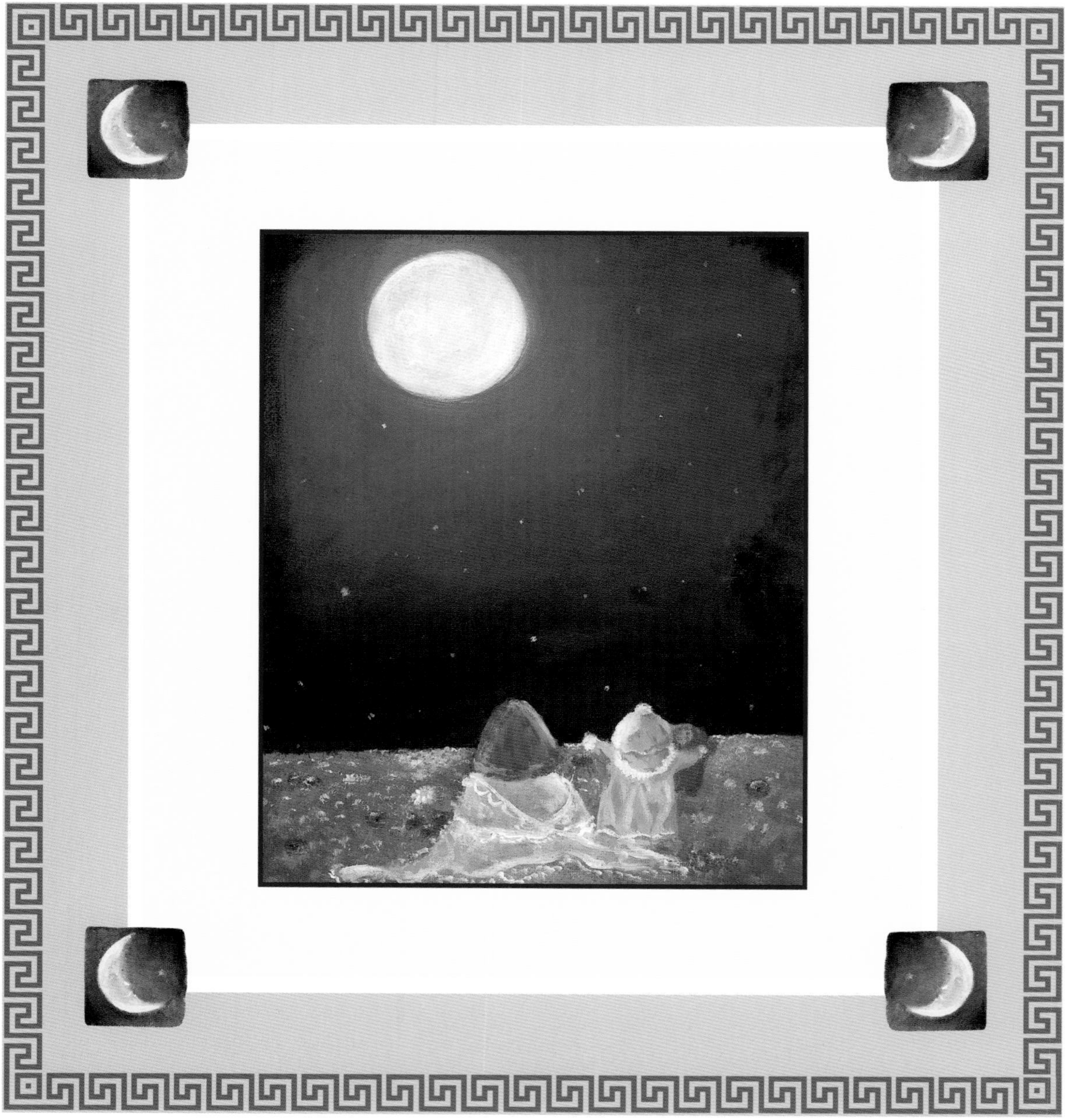

Moon & Stars

The moon has cast a spell on us for thousands of years. Before bedtime, take your little one to the window, or bundle up for an adventure outside, to say goodnight to the moon. Some nights, the moon will be full and shining bright; on others, only a small sliver will be seen. On clear nights, the stars will glimmer and add to the spectacle.

Bugs & Slugs

Every garden is full of winged bugs and tiny creatures. Your child can learn about insects and crawly things by carefully bringing them indoors for the day and observing them closely.

You and your little one can make a temporary bug home by placing some grass, a twig, and several drops of water in a see-through container with small holes poked in the top for air circulation. Creating a bug home is a wonderful opportunity to discuss the importance of insects in the garden and how careful we have to be when we have a pet— no matter how temporary. As the day is winding down, go out into the garden together and release the insect. As the sun dips, you can have fun saying good-bye and discussing what you learned together.

Creepy Crawling Friends

Name/Type	Date Found	Place Found

Notes

_____

_____

_____

_____

    3 4

Creepy Crawling Friends

Name/Type	Date Found	Place Found

Notes

Sounds

Take time throughout your day to stop with your child and listen to the sounds of the garden. Sit together on a garden bench or snuggle up in a chair for a moment of quiet listening. The natural world is full of music, from the chirping of birds and the rustle of the wind through the trees to the creaking sound of the garden gate and the gentle splash of rain as it lands in puddles.

Together you can duplicate some of the noises you hear in the garden. Try to repeat the buzz of the bees, the chirp of the crickets, and the singsong voices of the sparrows. You will be amazed at how quickly your child comes to recognize the distinct songs and calls of wildlife. When you draw attention to the sounds around you and your child, you deepen your relationship to the abundant life that makes a garden complete.

Colors

The garden is full of an amazing array of colors. Together you and your child can find yellow dandelions growing in the lawn, spy black crows flying overhead, and spot bright red ladybugs as they crawl across green leaves. Each flower, bird, and insect you see in the garden is an opportunity to teach your child about color and how it brightens our world. The more descriptive you are when presenting a blossom to your child, the more details your little one will notice and the deeper your child's appreciation of nature will become.

As you walk around the garden, listen to your little one talk about the plants and animals. Children have their favorite flowers and birds and their own whimsical pronunciations of names. Before you know it, your child will be pointing out special sights that you have overlooked.

Colors in the Garden

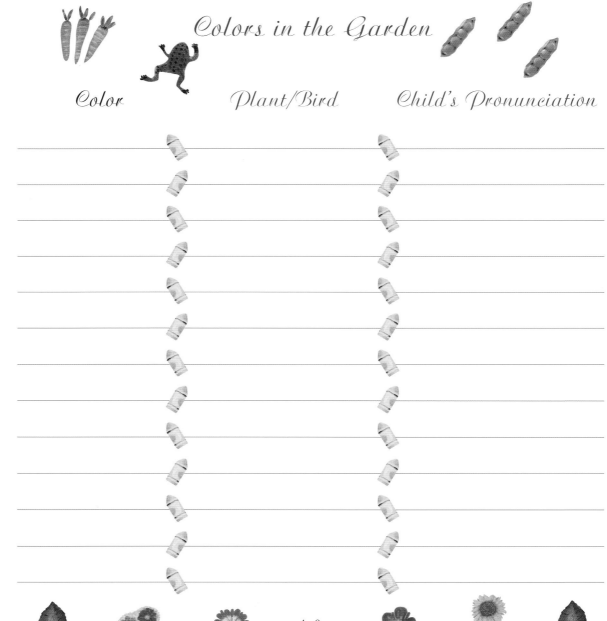

Color	Plant/Bird	Child's Pronunciation

40

Colors in the Garden

Color	Plant/Bird	Child's Pronunciation

Leaves

Fall is a wonderful time in the garden. As the weather cools and the days become shorter, the world around us begins a colorful transformation. When the leaves fall to the ground, rake together a small pile. Your child will have a fabulous time sitting in the pile, throwing leaves up in the air, and burrowing into a colorful new playground. While leaves are still strewn about the garden, make a game of marching around the yard with knees high and feet falling fast. Save some leaves from your adventures together and trace their images on paper. Your little one can then have the fun of coloring in each leaf and scribbling all over the page.

Snow

The first time a child sees snow is a magical experience. A blanket of white transforms the world the child has come to know so intimately. Bundle your little one up in a coat, hat, and mittens, and head outside. You and your child will delight in the icy cold snowflakes falling on your faces, the cold crisp taste of snow on your tongues, and the crunching sound of ice underfoot as you both move about. Together you can build a snowman, toss snowballs into the air, or simply go for a quiet walk around the winter garden.

Special Memories

Special Memories